D0486962

For Sam – JE

For Tilly – CF

First published in Great Britain in 2005
by Piccadilly Press Ltd,
5 Castle Road, London NW1 8PR
www.piccadillypress.co.uk

Designed by Christyan Fox
Printed and bound in China by WKT

ISBN: 1 85340 817 4 (hardback)
1 85340 822 0 (paperback)

1 3 5 7 9 10 8 6 4 2

A catalogue record of this book is available from the British Library

One Clever Creature

Joseph Ellis and Christyan Fox

Piccadilly Press • London

All around the world, animals do AMAZING things.

Some can swim,

others can fly,

some can
dig deep

or jump
really high.

But...

Goats can't paint pictures.

Frogs can't give hugs.

Tigers can't
hold hands.

Hippos can't wave.

Can a crocodile jump?

Can an elephant play hide and seek?

Can polar bears sing a song?

Can a penguin count to three?

A wolf can't blow out candles.

A cat can't bang a drum.

A dog can't clap along.

Or a tortoise climbing up the stairs?

Can you imagine a hen in your bath, washing her feathers with your best bubbly soap,

or a fox brushing
his teeth
before bed?

An owl can't
read a book.

A bat can't kiss
goodnight.

But would you believe me if I said I know a clever creature who CAN do all these things?

Well, there is one,
it's true. And this
clever creature is...